SAMURAI DEEPER
KYO

Vol. 2

by Akimine Kamijyo

Los Angeles • Tokyo • London

Translator - Takako Maeda
Additional Translation - Yukiko Nakamura & Dan Danko
English Adaptation - Dan Danko
Editor - Jake Forbes
Retouch and Lettering - Miyuki Ishihara
Cover Design - Aaron Suhr

Managing Editor - Jill Freshney
Production Coordinator - Antonio DePietro
Production Manager - Jennifer Miller
Art Director - Matthew Alford
Editorial Director - Jeremy Ross
VP of Production - Ron Klamert
President & C.O.O. - John Parker
Publisher & C.E.O. - Stuart Levy

Email: editor@TOKYOPOP.com
Come visit us online at www.TOKYOPOP.com

A TOKYOPOP® Manga
TOKYOPOP® is an imprint of Mixx Entertainment, Inc.
5900 Wilshire Blvd. Suite 2000, Los Angeles, CA 90036

ISBN: 1-59182-226-2

First TOKYOPOP® printing: August 2003

10 9 8 7 6 5 4 3 2 1

Printed in Canada

TABLE OF CONTENTS

Four years after the bloody Battle of Sekigahara, the paths of the mysterious medicine peddler, **Kyoshiro Mibu**, and the bounty huntress, **Yuya Shiina**, happened to cross.

Yuya soon realized there was much more to her companion than meets the eye.

The peaceful Kyoshiro... And the legendary samurai, Demon Eyes Kyo.

Two spirits trapped in one body:

I THINK WE SHOULD GO THIS WAY.

The two travel west, each in pursuit of their own goal...

ONE MILLION RYO BOUNTY FOR KYO. 100 MON FOR KYOSHIRO.
I'LL USE MY FEMININE WILES TO SUBDUE HIM! THEN I'LL HAVE ALL THE MONEY I NEED TO HUNT DOWN THE MAN WITH THE SCAR.

At Ochiudo Village, swordsman **Jimon** started massacring the fugitive samurai.

Including Mika's father who hoped to delay Jimon long enough for his daughter to escape.

Kyoshiro confronted Jimon as he attacked Mika. He gave Jimon an ominous warning...

"Stop now..."

...OR **HE** WILL COME.

SAMURAI DEEPER KYO

CHAPTER 6
DEPTH

For cultural notes, consult the glossary on page 196.

HEH HEH HEH... WELL THEN, C'MON...

I'M WAITING, *DEMON EYES KYO.*

BUT DEMON EYES KYO IS SO SHY!

HE'LL BE SO EMBARRASSED WITH ALL THESE PEOPLE WATCHING!

WAH! HE HE HE!
AH HA HA!
HA... HA...
HA HA HA HA HA HA!
HA HA HA HA HA HA!

GO TO HELL!
KYOSHIRO!
GUH!
ARE YOU OKAY?
GET OUT OF HERE, YUYA-SAN!
WHAT?

I'M TRYING TO HOLD HIM BACK, BUT I CAN'T DO IT FOR LONG. YOU'VE SEEN WHAT HAPPENS WHEN HE COMES!

I'LL HOLD OFF JIMON FOR AS LONG AS I CAN! GET THESE PEOPLE OUT OF HERE!

...

...
TELL ME WHERE THE HELL KYO IS!
You'll find your peace in the grave.
PLEASE ...

KUH!
?!
INDULGE ME...

GUH!

DRAW YOUR SWORD, OR DIE.

CA... CAN'T WE TALK ABOUT THIS ...?

YOU WOULD MOCK ME?!

DRAW YOUR SWORD, DAMN YOU!

GUH!

tee hee hee
DO IT! DO IT!
AGH!
hee hee
HE CAN NOT...
HE WILL NOT DRAW IT. tee hee
HE WON'T LAST MUCH LONGER.
BUT IF KYOSHIRO DIES... WHAT OF KYO?

YOU'RE NOT SO TOUGH.

DAMN IT, KID! I BRUISED A KNUCKLE.

Why'd you have to be so stubborn?

UGH!

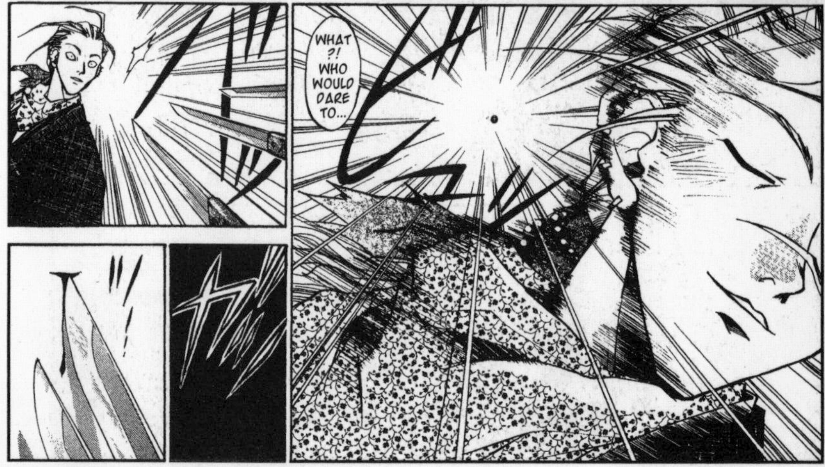

DAMN! HE CAUGHT THEM!

YOU DIDN'T THINK I'D LET YOU HOG ALL THE ACTION, DID YOU, KYOSHIRO!

SHOULD I KILL YOU FIRST, THEN?
GIRL ...
...
YUYA-SAN... RUN!

NOT SO FAST, SAMURAI. WE'LL SEE YOU DEAD FIRST!
YOU'VE INVADED OUR HOME. THIS IS *OUR* FIGHT, NOT THEIRS.
E... EVERY-BODY...
YOU THINK I CAME HERE FOR YOU SHIT OCHIUDO?
BUT IF YOU INSIST...

!!

EVERY-BODY! RUN!

IF HE COMES, HE'LL KILL YOU ALL!

LISTEN TO ME, DAMN YOU!

GET THE HELL OUT OF HERE!

WHY DO YOU CARE ABOUT THESE STINKING PEASANTS? YOU MAKE ME SICK!

UH WAH!

WHAT DO YOU THINK OF THIS PROPOSITION...

UNTIL YOU DRAW YOUR SWORD, I'LL KILL THEM ALL— ONE... BY... ONE...

WHY?

WHY DO YOU SPREAD SUCH HATRED?

THE WAR IS OVER!
WHY DO YOU HAVE TO KEEP KILLING PEOPLE?!
ONE HUNDRED AND SEVEN.
?!
ONE HUNDRED AND SEVEN PEOPLE I KILLED TO PERFECT MY TECHNIQUE. IT WAS FLAWED... CRUDE...
THE PEOPLE I KILLED WERE WORTHLESS SCUM... PERFECT FOR TARGET PRACTICE.
Heh-heh...
THIS GUY'S NUTS ...

AND THEN IT WAS AS IF A SHROUD WAS PULLED BACK FROM THE SUN... AND FOR THE FIRST TIME... I COULD SEE!
...
...
HA HA HA... I COULD SEE ALL THE SECRETS THE SWORD HELD FROM ME FOR SO LONG. EVERYTHING BECAME SO... CLEAR...
AAA AH...
THAT'S THE ONLY REASON I BECAME A YOJIMBO TO THAT SHIT DAIKAN.
AA...
AAAAA...
HE GAVE ME PLENTY OF PRACTICE, PRACTICE, PRACTICE... SO MANY DEAD!
...
AND NOW YOU...
...SHALL BE THE ONE HUNDRED AND EIGHTH!
THIS TIME, YOU WILL BE THE ONE HUMILIATED, DEMON EYES KYO!
HEH HEH HEH...
HA HA HA HA!
YOU...

YOU KILLED ALL THOSE PEOPLE FOR PRACTICE ?!
ばっ

YOU'RE NO SAMURAI! YOU'RE NOT EVEN A MAN!
SOB!
YOU'RE JUST AN ANIMAL WHO DOESN'T EVEN KNOW HOW TO LOVE!

OH... I KNOW LOVE.

DEATH IS MY LOVER. THE KATANA IS MADE TO KILL, AND BY RIGHTS AS A SAMURAI, I AM PRIVILEGED TO KILL ANYONE.

SHOULD I NOT EXERCISE MY RIGHTS?

YOU SHIT!
YOU MAKE ME SICK!
...

NOW ...
DRAW YOUR SWORD AND FIGHT!

……
YOU'RE NOTHING COMPARED TO KYO.
YOU'RE SUCH A FOOL...
?!
WHAT?!

HEH HEH HEH... IF I AM NOTHING ...

...THEN YOU...

...ARE LESS THAN NOTHING.

KYO-SHIRO!
NO! YOU'LL BE...

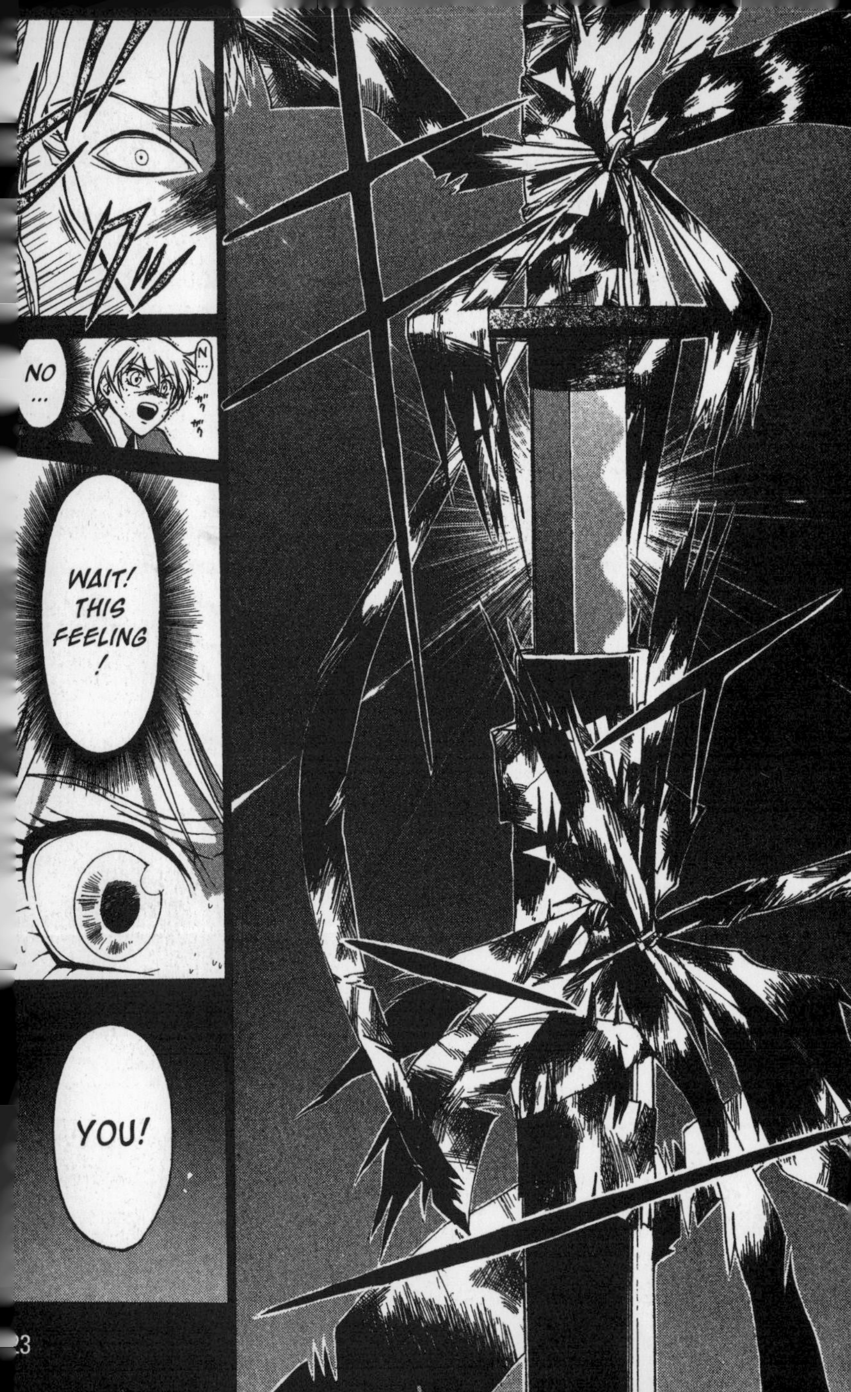
N...
NO...
WAIT! THIS FEELING!
YOU!

YOU JUST COULDN'T STOP, COULD YOU?
GUH!
AT LAST!
HEH HEH HEH ...

ギリ
ギリ
YOU GOT WHAT YOU WANTED. YOU WOKE ME UP.
AT LAST WE MEET!
HE CAME! HE FINALLY CAME!
tee hee hee
OH HELL! WE'RE IN FOR IT NOW...
ゴク…
ザッ

DEMON EYES...
I'M IN A SHITTY MOOD WHEN I WAKE UP.
SAMURAI ...
KYO!
YOU DO REALIZE... YOU'RE GOING TO DIE?

I'M IN A SHITTY MOOD WHEN I WAKE UP.

DEMON EYES KYO!

YOU DO REALIZE YOU'RE GOING TO DIE?

SAMURAI DEEPER KYO

CHAPTER 7 SECRET WAY OF THE SWORD

WHO THE HELL ARE YOU?

?!

WHAT?!

YOU...YOU DON'T REMEMBER ME?! YOU GAVE ME *IKIHAJI* AT SEKIGAHARA, LEFT ME IN DISGRACE.

...

...!

AAAAH!

NOW, YOU RE-MEM-BER!

NO, I DON'T REMEMBER YOU.

I JUST REALIZED WHAT AN IDIOT YOU REALLY ARE.

W... WHAT... Y...
YOU...!
HEY, GIRL!
HUH?!
IT'S NOT THAT EASY, KYO!
W... WHAT?
DID YOU FIND THAT GUY WITH THE SCAR ON HIS BACK?
おず
ISN'T IT?
WHAT?!
WHAT YOU LOOK FOR MIGHT BE CLOSER THAN YOU EXPECT.
MUCH CLOSER...
WHAT?
WHAT DO YOU MEAN?
THAT'S HIM!

THE LEGENDARY ONE MILLION RYO BOUNTY, DEMON EYES KYO IS HERE!
BRING ME HIS HEAD!
A BAG OF GOLD TO THE MAN WHO DOES THE JOB!
YAAA!

EH?
AEEEE!!!
J-JIMON?! H-HOW COULD YOU?!
DEMON EYES KYO IS **MINE**, FAT MAN.
WHAT?!
...
YOU WORK FOR ME, YOU JACKASS SAMURAI! YOU'RE SUPPOSED TO PROTECT ME!
PROTECT YOU?
YOU ARE THE ONE WHO ROBS, WHO KILLS, WHO RAPES.
IT'S THE OCHIUDO AND THEIR FAMILIES WHO NEED THE PROTECTION, YOU PIG OF A DAIKAN.
NO!
THAT IS A...
...LIE!

OUR SUFFER-ING...IS YOUR FAULT?
YOU'RE WORSE...
...THAN A PIG!
NO! HE LIES! I COME FROM A GREAT BUKE! I WOULD NEVER--!
My men are the selfish ones...
TELL IT TO SOMEONE WHO CARES, FAT MAN.
AT LAST...
AT LAST... AT LAST...
あ
あ
AT LAST... AT LAST...
AT LAST...
AT LAST...
AT LAST...
AT LAST...

VENGEANCE IS MINE...
...DEMON EYES KYO!
SO FAST!
?!
WHY DOESN'T HE MOVE?!
I'VE GOT HIM!

HA HA HA... YOU'RE QUICK. BUT I'M JUST WARMING UP.

WHAT A COINCI-DENCE...

SO AM I.

WHAT?
!!
JUST WARMING UP!? THEY'RE SO FAST I DIDN'T EVEN SEE THEM MOVE!
AMAZING!
GOOD...
GOOD... GOOD... GOOD... GOOD...
I WOULDN'T HAVE IT ANY OTHER WAY.
NOW I WILL SHOW YOU THE ONE AND ONLY TECHNIQUE DEVISED TO...
...KILL YOU!
?!

COME...
...DEMON EYES KYO!
?!
WHAT?! JIMON SHEATHED HIS SWORD! WHAT'S HE DOING?!
......

SO...WHAT DO YOU THINK OF MY TECHNIQUE? IT'S CALLED **HIEN KEN**.

WHAT?!

H-HOW ON EARTH DID THAT HAPPEN?!

AMAZING! HE'S MASTERED HIEN KEN!
WHAT DO YOU MEAN?

HIEN KEN...FLYING SPARROW...THE SPEED OF THE GODS! A SAMURAI WHO KNOWS SUCH TECHNIQUE CAN UNSHEATH A SWORD AND STRIKE THREE TIMES IN THE BLINK OF AN EYE!
THEY SAY THE STYLE VANISHED BECAUSE IT WAS IMPOSSIBLE TO MASTER!

WHAT?
JIMON CAN STRIKE KYO DOWN BEFORE HE EVEN SEES THE BLADE!
KYO WILL BE KILLED WITH ONE BLOW!
YES... WITH THE QUICKNESS HE CLOSES THEIR MAAI...
...HE'S TRULY INVINCIBLE!

THERE'S NO... ...HOPE...
NOTH-ING!
THERE'S NOTHING KYO CAN DO!
HA HA HA...NOW YOU KNOW MY HUMILIATION ...
THIS TIME...
...YOU SHALL BE THE HELPLESS ONE!
THIS TIME, I WILL LOOK DOWN UPON YOU...
...LIKE A BUG.
A TINY, HELPLESS BUG.
I...
DON'T WORRY. I'LL END YOUR SUFFERING QUICKLY...
SHLIP
HEH HEH HEH!

I... I...I... HA HA HA HA HA!
ゲラ
ゲラ
DON'T MAKE ME LAUGH!
ゲラ
HIEN KEN, HUH?
IT'S JUST...
...DRAWING A SWORD.
Why try to act so cool?

ONCE MORE...
C'MON...
LET'S SEE WHO'S THE FASTER DRAW.

A WHAT?
IT'S A DUEL TO SEE WHO CAN DRAW HIS BLADE FASTER.
JIMON'S IAI-STYLE SWORD USES THE SAYA BASHIRI TECHNIQUE TO GAIN SPEED AND POWER FROM THE ACT OF UNSHEATHING.
BUT, KYO...HE HAS NO SHEATH! HE'LL SLICE OFF HIS OWN HAND!
AND THAT SWORD! IT'S TOO LONG! HE'LL NEVER DRAW IT FASTER THAN JIMON!
HE'S USING THE IAI STANCE...?! A DRAWING MATCH?!
HE CAN'T WIN!
NO!
C'MON, KYO. MAKE YOUR MOVE...
...OR SHOULD I KILL YOU BEFORE YOU BLINK?
WHAT ARE YOU THINKING, KYO?
HAVE YOU MADE YOUR FINAL PEACE YET, HMMM?
GO ON...
GIVE IT A TRY.

WELL, WELL...WHAT TROUBLE HAVE YOU MADE FOR YOURSELF NOW, KYO? YOU SEEM TO LIKE IT...
So macho...
AND SO DO I.
tee hee hee
IT'S ALL SO EXCITING!
I HOPE THERE'S BLOOD! I LOVE THE COLOR RED...

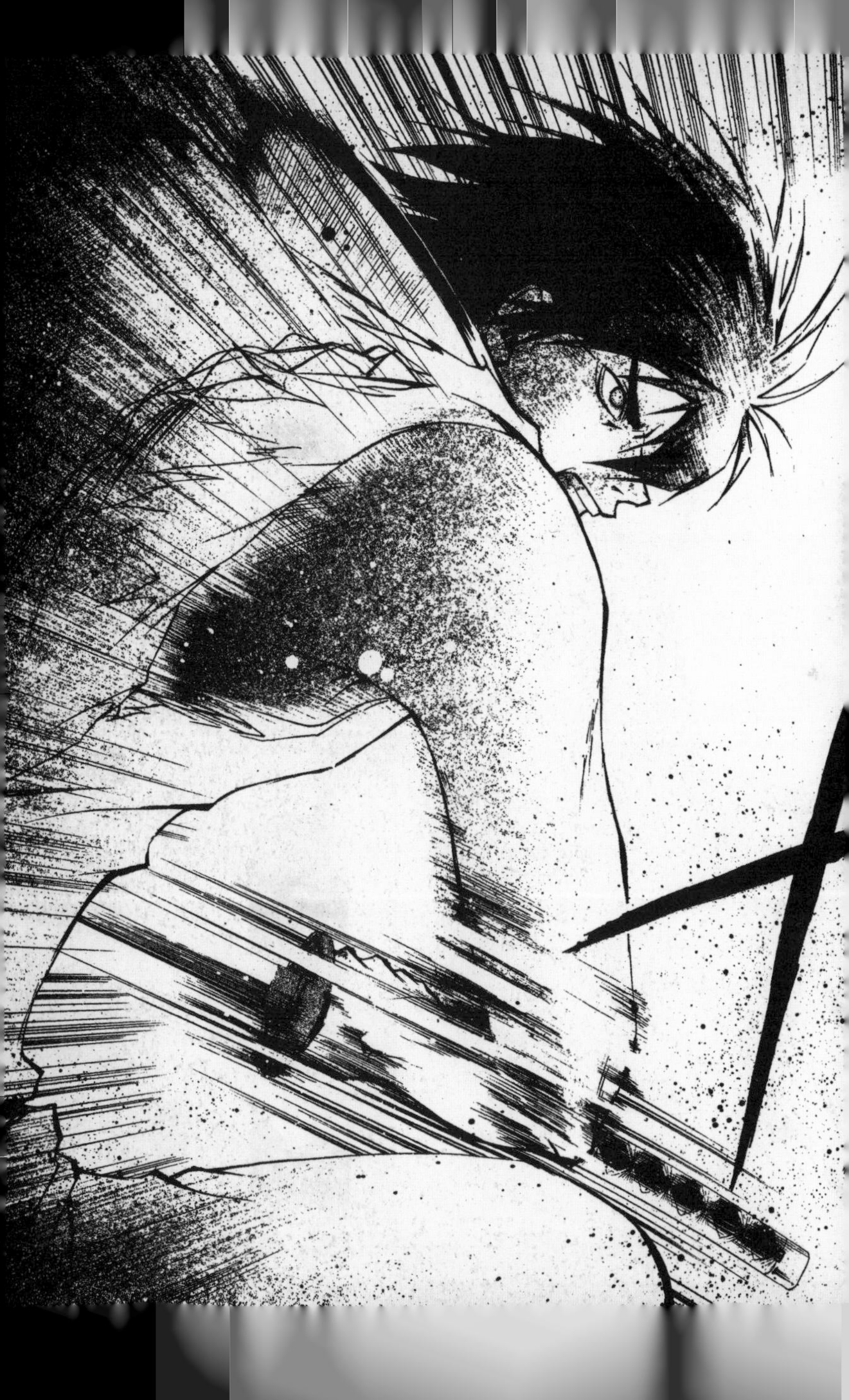

Three Color Gang completed

BABUKO WAS GIVEN TO ME BY MR. S.

I JUST HAVE TO GIVE IT WATER AND IT'LL GROW BY ITSELF. WE HAVE A LOT IN COMMON, SO WE'RE GETTING ALONG JUST FINE.

IT'S MY ONLY PARTNER NOW.

SAMURAI DEEPER KYO

CHAPTER 8
LEGENDARY FORCE

CRAP. KYO HAS TO WIN!

I'VE WON!
HE DIDN'T EVEN DRAW HIS SWORD!
I'VE BEAT YOU...

...KYO!

NO ONE... ...IS FASTER...
...THAN...
...ME.
OF COURSE NOT.
THE STRONG ARE STRONG...
...AND THE WEAK ARE DEAD.
AMAZING!
HE LET JIMON DRAW FIRST... AND STILL WON!

THIS IS...!

...THE LEGENDARY FORCE... THE KILLER OF A THOUSAND MEN.

YOU WAITED ALL THIS TIME... AND THAT'S IT?!

HOW DULL.

YAAA!

RUN AWAY!

...

WAIT...

LET'S TALK.

...

...

GYAAAH!

?!

HEY!

THERE YOU GO. THIS IS TWICE I SAVED YOU.

I NEVER ASKED FOR YOUR HELP!

AND DON'T PRETEND YOU GIVE A DAMN ABOUT ME!

もみ
!!
もみ
HMM. ALL THIS SHOUTING WILL STUNT YOUR GROWTH.
WHAT?! WHY YOU--!
IT'S TRUE. YOU NEED TO RELAX. I DON'T THINK IT'S TOO LATE.
I'm just trying to be kind.
UNLESS, OF COURSE, YOU LIKE THEM THAT--
SHUT UP!
DON'T YOU AGREE?
WHAT?
WHO'RE YOU TALKING TO?
OKUNI ?!

WHAT THE HELL HAPPENED TO YOU?! I WAS WORRIED YOU'D--
......
すっ
HUH ?
WHAT?! WHAT'S GOTTEN INTO HER?!
YOU HAVEN'T CHANGED A BIT, KYO.
THE CRUEL EYES. THE COLD SMILE. EVERY-THING...
......
... EXACTLY AS I REMEM-BERED THEM.
WAIT A SECOND ...

WHAT DID KYO SAY TO ME...
COULD OKUNI BE...
IT MAY PLEASE YOU TO KNOW...
...THAT YOU'RE ONLY THE SECOND PERSON THAT I'VE SPARED
KYOSHIRO WAS WRONG. YOU'RE STILL THE SAME, DEMON EYES KYO. BUT PERHAPS...
...A SMALL TEST?
NO. NOTHING'S CHANGED.

WHO SENT YOU THIS TIME, *BITCH?*
IT'S ALWAYS THE SAME. *INFORMANTS* LIKE YOU ARE NOTHING BUT TROUBLE.
AND YOU'RE AS SCHEMING AS THEY COME.
I'LL BET YOU'RE THE ONE WHO TOLD THE GENERAL WHERE THE OCHIUDO WERE HIDING.
WHY, OKUNI? IS YOUR HUNGER FOR BLOOD SO GREAT?

WHY WOULD YOU SAY SUCH A THING?
IF YOU THINK SO LITTLE OF ME...
...THEN TELL ME TO LEAVE.
Right?
EH?
FUUU...

HE STILL LIVES, KYO...

HE LIVES... AND HE HATES... YOU.

?!
HUH?
TELL ME...
...OKUNI...
TELL ME...
...WHERE HE IS--NOW!

I...I CAN'T BREATHE!
I'VE NEVER FELT SO S...
AH... AHH...
DEMON EYES KYO... HE'S SO...
UH...
...SCARED...

TSK, TSK... TEMPER, TEMPER!
Scary, scary!
SO YOU WANT TO KNOW?
Heh heh heh
OKAY, BUT I GET A FAVOR, FIRST!

...
SHE'S... SHE'S FLOATING!
LET'S SEE...WHAT DO I WANT? I KNOW! HOW ABOUT... YOUR HEAD?
Tee hee hee!
ケラ ケラ ケラ
GO TO HELL!

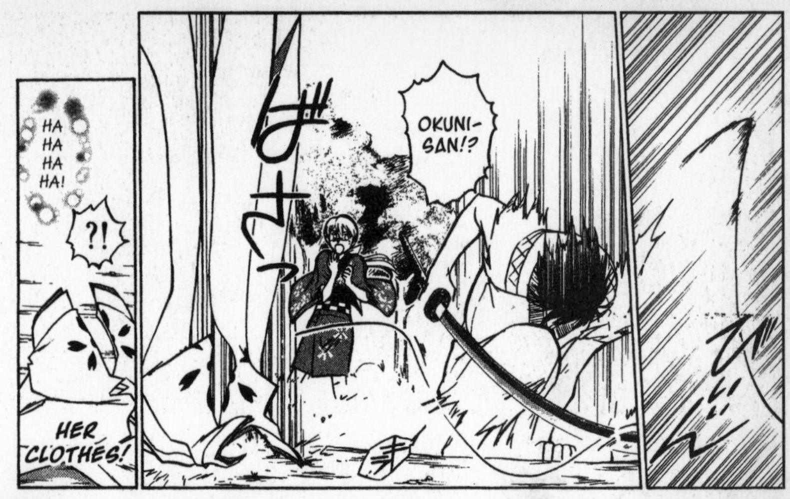

OKUNI-SAN!?
HA HA HA HA!
?!
HER CLOTHES!

ALWAYS WITH THE TEMPER!
!!

WOMEN DON'T LIKE TO BE ROUGHED UP.
KYO-SAN...
Until next time, keep working!

WE'LL MEET AGAIN...

OKUNI COULDN'T BE THE FIRST PERSON KYO SPARED.
I DON'T THINK HE COULD KILL HER IF HE TRIED! Who is she?
SUCH POWER ...

WHAT DOES SHE KNOW ABOUT HIS PAST? AND WHO IS THE **"HE"** SHE REFERRED TO THAT MADE HIM SO MAD?

カチャン
カチャン
カチャン
カチャン

KYOSHIRO...
SO DIFFERENT FROM KYO. SO QUIET...
WH-AT...
WHAT'S HE THINKING...?

I WONDER WHERE MIKA AND THE OTHERS ARE NOW.
HOPE THEY FIND THE PEACE THEY SEEK.

SO WHAT ARE YOU GOING TO DO NOW?
WE HAVE TO MOVE AGAIN...
THIS TIME, TO A PLACE FAR FROM THE WORLD'S EYES.
YES ...
BUT IT'S OKAY.

THIS TIME ...
...I FINALLY UNDERSTAND WHAT'S MOST IMPORTANT TO ME.

MIKA-CHAN ...
THANKS TO YOU TWO, WE'LL ALL BE FINE.
AND KYOSHIRO'S MEDICINE, OF COURSE!
Dad's better already!
わっはは
AH-HA HA HA HA HA HA!
That medicine works?
PLEASE TAKE CARE...
That stuff still might make it worse.
YUYA-SAN...

IF YOU SEE KYO AGAIN, TELL HIM THANKS FOR THE HELP...
WHAT?!
I CAN'T TELL HIM THAT!
HE DIDN'T CARE ABOUT SAVING YOU...
DIDN'T HE?
WHAT?!
?!
THANK YOU VERY MUCH.
AT SEKIGAHARA, HE CLEARED A PATH TO SAFETY THROUGH THE ENEMY RANKS.
SO?! HE DID IT TO SAVE HIS OWN HIDE!
MAYBE. MAYBE NOT.
EITHER WAY, HE SAVED MY HIDE AS WELL.
SO TELL HIM THANK YOU. BECAUSE OF HIM, I CAN PROTECT MY DAUGHTER...
...AGAIN.

I DON'T GET IT!
C'MON! LET'S HAVE SOME FUN!
WHO WANTS TO DIE NEXT?
KYO ISN'T JUST A MURDERER?!
WHAT'S THE TRUTH?
WHAT IS KYO REALLY LIKE?
FINALLY... I'VE DECIDED.
?!
WHAT IS IT, KYO-SHIRO?! WHAT?!

I COULDN'T DECIDE! YUKINO-CHAN OR AYAME-CHAN?

BUT I'VE CHOSEN AYAME-CHAN!

She's my kind of Comfort Girl. And she's got the biggest breasts!

SAMURAI DEEPER KYO
COME BACK HERE!
YOU CAN'T ESCAPE!
CHAPTER 9
YUYA MEETS THE PICKPOCKETS
HA HA! YOU DON'T EXPECT HEISUKE OF IDATEN TO GIVE UP TO A BOUNTY HUNTER LIKE YOU, DO YOU?
NOW, KYO-SHIRO!
ガコン ガコン
?!

WHY IS IT ALWAYS MEEEEEEEE?!
YAAAAAA!

I'VE GOT A NICE CELL FOR YOU! Otsukare-san!
YES! Otsukare-sama!
HEE HEE HEE
Y'KNOW, IF YOU CATCH ENOUGH OF THEM, EVEN THESE LITTLE BOUNTIES...
...START TO ADD UP!
HUH?!

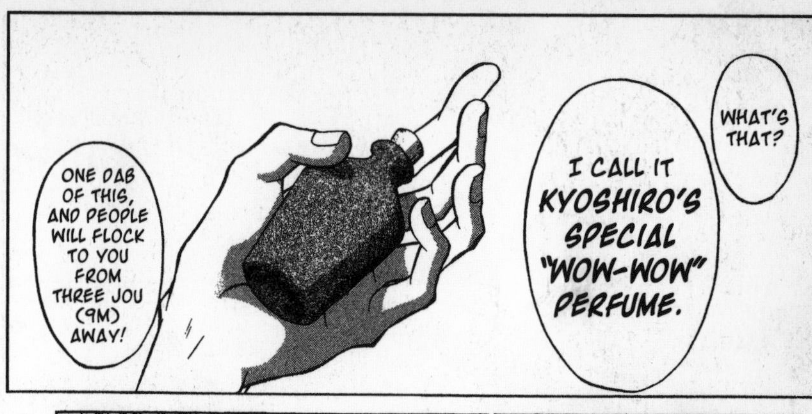

WHAT'S THAT?
I CALL IT KYOSHIRO'S SPECIAL "WOW-WOW" PERFUME.
ONE DAB OF THIS, AND PEOPLE WILL FLOCK TO YOU FROM THREE JOU (9M) AWAY!

I CAN'T SELL IT, THOUGH. IT'S JUST TOO POWERFUL.
And different.
WHO'D EVER USE THIS STUFF?
. . .
BUT I'LL GIVE IT TO YOU, YUYA-SAN, AS A SPECIAL GIFT.
Use it! Use it!
GEE... THANKS ...

HMMM... IT WOULD BE SO EASY...
But that damn Kyo is still the real prize.
I REALLY THINK YOU'LL LIKE THE SCENT.
Have you seen this face?
BOUNTY #110!!!
Wanted: For not paying tavern bill
Mibu, Kyoshiro
- Height: 5' 8"
- Young age
- Wears white Kinagashi
- Travelling medicine seller
- May be dangerous
100 Mon!
Raised 200 mon!
BE ON THE LOOK-OUT!!

SO... ANY IDEA WHERE WE SHOULD STAY TONIGHT?

I DON'T WANT TO CAMP OUT AGAIN... EVER.

WOULD THERE EVEN BE A HOTEL IN A TOWN THIS SMALL?

THIS TOWN WAS RANSACKED DURING SEKIGAHARA. NO WONDER-- IT WAS RIGHT IN THE WARPATH OF THE TOUGUN.

IT STILL LOOKS LIKE A GHOST TOWN...

HEY! ONII-CHAN!

HUH?

GIVE ME SOMETHING!

I'M SORRY, LITTLE GUY, I REALLY DON'T HAVE ANYTHING TO...

GIM-ME!

GIM-ME!

GIM-ME!
GIM-ME!
わら
HUH?
WAIT ... WAIT!
わら
GIM-ME!
GIM-ME!
わら
...
KYO-SHIRO ...?
WA AAA AA!

LEAVE ME ALONE!

YOU'RE JUST A KID...

LEAVE MY BROTHER ALONE!
KOUTA'S NOT BAD!
HE'S NOT BAD! KOUTA WAS TOLD TO--
HUH?
SHIT, TAE! SHUT UP!
SHUT YOUR MOUTH OR I'LL DO IT FOR YOU!
UH...
UH...
DON'T CRY, STUPID!
UH...
C'MON, YOU STUPID LITTLE...
LOOK! I'M OKAY, RIGHT? THEY DIDN'T HURT ME!
UH...
GOT IT?!

HOW AM I SUPPOSED TO SURVIVE, HUH?
...
THE SAMURAI KILLED OUR PARENTS! SOMEBODY'S GOT TO BE THE MAN IN THIS FAMILY AND PUT FOOD ON THE TABLE. I CAN'T LET MY SISTER STARVE.
YOU REALLY WANNA HELP ME?
And my sister.
THEN STOP SMILING AND GIVE ME SOME MONEY SO WE CAN EAT!

GNHH...

?!

I DON'T NEED YOUR PITY.

I'M NOT OFFERING YOU PITY...

I'M OFFERING YOU A JOB. CARRY OUR BAGS TO A HOTEL.

I'M NOT GONNA DO WHAT YOU TELL ME!
TAE'S NOT THE STUPID ONE, KOUTA. YOU SHOULD BE OLD ENOUGH...
...TO KNOW THE DIFFERENCE BETWEEN INTEGRITY AND STUBBORNNESS. BUT IF YOU DON'T, ASK YOURSELF...
...WHO AM I REALLY HELPING?
MY PRIDE...
...OR THE ONES I LOVE?

AH! BUTTER-FLY!
BUTTER-FLY! BUTTER-FLY!
WHO AM I REALLY HELPING?
MY PRIDE...OR THE ONES I LOVE?

...
HEY, KOUTA ...
WHAT KEPT YOU? YOU'RE LATE.

KAZURA NEE-SAN...
...IS WAITING FOR TODAY'S TAKE.
LET'S GO.

LOOK! I'M OKAY, RIGHT? THEY DIDN'T HURT ME!
GOT IT?!
UH...

THAT REMINDS ME...
SO LONG AGO...

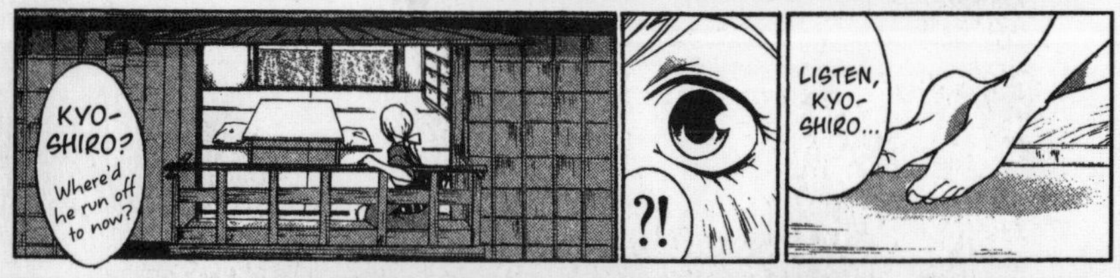
LISTEN, KYO-SHIRO...
?!
KYO-SHIRO? Where'd he run off to now?

かっ ゆ ぽ〜ん

*BATH

SO NICE …

WHATTA BODY!
HER FACE IS SO YOUNG, BUT THAT BODY IS ALL WOMAN!
I'LL BET HER MEASUREMENTS ARE BUST: 3 SHAKU 1 SUN 3 BU; WAIST: 1 SHAKU 9 SUN, 8 BU; HIPS: 2 SHAKU, 8 SUN, 3 BU! (36-24-36)

HA!
HA!
HA!
OH WHATTA NIGHT! SO MANY BEAUTIFUL WOMEN AND SUCH TINY TOWELS!
I'm so lucky I found this!
HA!
HA!

やっほ
AAAH!
AAAH!
YOU HAVE BEAUTIFUL SKIN...
REALLY?

WOW! THIS ONE'S GOT A BODY LIKE A MOUNTAIN ROAD...
SHE'S GOTTA BE BUST: 2 SHAKU 6 SUN 9 BU; WAIST: 1 SHAKU 8 SUN 1 BU; HIPS: 2 SHAKU 7 SUN! (34-22-32)
NOTHING BUT CURVES AND MOUNDS!

?!
OKAY! WHO'S NEXT?
AH HH HH!

TIME TO RELIEVE AN OLD WOMAN'S BLADDER ...

H...HELP ME... I'm scarred for life!

YEAH, YEAH, MOVE ALONG, OLD BAG!
I BETTER GET BACK BEFORE YUYA-SAN COMES.
But just one more look!

THEY'RE GOING TO KILL ONII-TAN.

THEY'LL DO IT!

PLEASE HELP, ONEE-TAN!

ドカッ
バキッ

GUH!
DO YOU STILL FEEL THAT WAY?
NO!
AAAH!
I DON'T WANT TO PICK-POCKET ANY MORE!

DAMN BRAT!
STOP!
SIGH... SUCH BARBARIANS.
IS THIS THE WAY I TAUGHT YOU TO BEHAVE?
WELL, KOUTA...
WHY DO YOU MAKE MY MEN DO THIS TO YOU?

WHAT ARE YOU THINKING, KOUTA? HMMM?
HAVE YOU FORGOTTEN WHO TOOK YOU IN AFTER YOUR PARENTS DIED? Don't say you want to quit.
I APPRECIATE WHAT YOU DID FOR TAE AND ME...
BUT ...
I DON'T WANT TO PICK-POCKET ANY MORE!
I WANNA GO STRAIGHT!
I'M IMPRESSED ...

SUCH BRAVE WORDS!
GYAAAAAH!

WHO PICKED YOU OUT OF THE GUTTER AND FED YOU? WHO TAUGHT YOU TO MAKE A LIVING AND GAVE YOU LOVE?
AND YOU WOULD DARE TURN YOUR BACK ON ME?!
AAAAH!
GGG GUH ...
A... AA AA ...
OH!
I'LL ASK YOU AGAIN ...
WILL YOU PICK-POCKET ?
NO!

FOOLISH TWAT!
OKAY, BOYS, CUT HIM.
YES!
STOP!
WAAAH!
THEN THROW HIM OUT...
...SO HE CAN STARVE WITH HIS SISTER.
GAAAH!
WHAT?!
WHO THE HELL ARE YOU?!

SO, I WAS WRONG. IT'S NOT SOME DUMB JERK USING THESE KIDS...
...IT'S A STUPID BITCH.
Disgusting job for a woman...
WHO ARE YOU!?
NII-TAN!
I'M THE BOUNTY HUNTRESS, YUYA SHIINA.
BOUNTY HUNTRESS?!
KOUTA!
NE... NEE-CHAN... I DID MY BEST...
BUT ...
SHHH. I KNOW.
YOU DID TERRIFIC.
WHAT THE HELL ARE YOU DOING HERE?! THERE'S NO BOUNTIES FOR US!

YOU KNOW, LADY...I GET THE FEELING...

...YOU'RE ONE JOB I'LL DO FOR FREE.

Mean-while ...

UH... YUYA-SAN...YOU FORGOT TO...

Kyoshiro's role

Taiwanese Version

We decided to publish a Taiwa-nese version of "Kyo."
It'll be the same story, just translated into Taiwanese.
What?!
Wow! Publishing comics is easy, huh?

IT JUST DOESN'T SEEM RIGHT...

Did they really say **"lucky"** in the 16th century?!
Samurai had armor like that?!
Wow! That girl's got **permed hair**!
They had **guns** back then?!
Samurai had **short hair**?!
TAIWANESE KIDS
TAIWAN EDITION
JAPAN SURE WAS A STRANGE PLACE...
Just imagine what they'll think if this thing gets published in America...

While traveling, Yuya and Kyoshiro met the two young orphan pickpockets, **Kouta** and **Tae**. Yuya convinced Kouta to give up stealing.

Tae fled and finally found Yuya.

But, **Kazura**, the pickpocket ringleader, wasn't eager to let Kouta quit.

WHAT THE HELL ARE YOU DOING HERE?! THERE'S NO BOUNTIES FOR US!

NE... NEE-CHAN...I DID MY BEST... BUT ...
SHHH. I KNOW.

YOU KNOW, LADY...I GET THE FEELING...

...YOU'RE ONE JOB I'LL DO FOR FREE.

SAMURAI DEEPER
KYO
CHAPTER 10
YUYA: NOT
FIGHTING, DANCING

DON'T MESS WITH US, BITCH!
WA AA AH!
MA AA MA!

DIE!
?!

GYAH!
WHAT ARE YOU DOING? GET HER!
SHE MAY HAVE A GUN, BUT SHE'S STILL JUST A GIRL!
JUST A GIRL WITH A GUN, HUH?
SO, HOW ABOUT THIS?
?!

GUNH!
GUUU!
GWAH!

ACK!
GAAH!

UUUUUH...
!
YUYA SHIINA?! I KNOW THAT NAME!

LAST YEAR YOU TOOK DOWN KUBI KIRI OTORAMARU, THE DECAPITATOR!
YOU ONLY GO AFTER THE BIGGEST BOUNTIES, AND STILL YOUR CAPTURE RATIO IS ALMOST 100%! YOU'RE A LEGEND!

ARE YOU REALLY YUYA SHIINA?!

ARE YOU ...
NEXT ...
YOUR NUMBER'S UP.
AE EII!

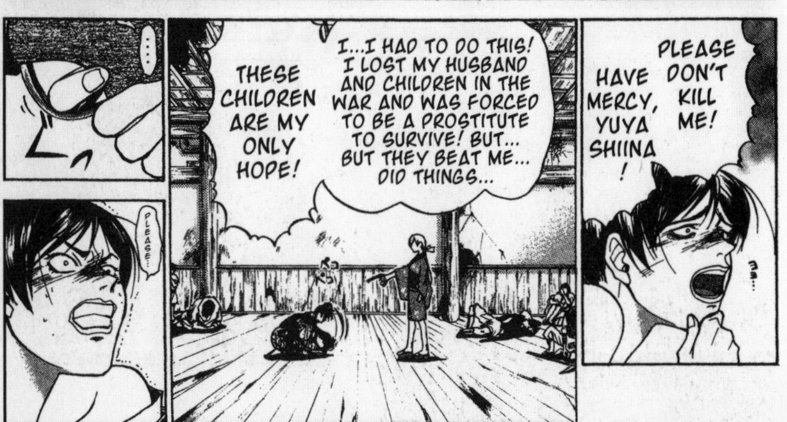

PLEASE DON'T KILL ME!
HAVE MERCY, YUYA SHIINA!
I...I HAD TO DO THIS! I LOST MY HUSBAND AND CHILDREN IN THE WAR AND WAS FORCED TO BE A PROSTITUTE TO SURVIVE! BUT... BUT THEY BEAT ME... DID THINGS...
THESE CHILDREN ARE MY ONLY HOPE!
...
PLEASE...

KOUTA! TELL HER! TELL HER HOW I LOVED YOU AND CARED FOR YOU!
AHH!
YOU CAN TELL HER, KOUTA!
TELL HER HOW YOU AND TAE WERE ALMOST DEAD WHEN I FOUND YOU!
TELL HER EVERY-THING I DID FOR YOU!

...
WELL DONE, KOUTA! YOU KNOW YOU'RE MY FAVORITE...
I SWEAR.
TELL ME WHAT YOU WANT KOUTA, AND I'LL BUY IT FOR YOU!
PLEASE...PLEASE...

NEE-CHAN ...
... PLEASE FORGIVE HER!
KOUTA!
SHE ISN'T ALWAYS GOOD, BUT SHE DID SAVE ME AND TAE!

ARE YOU SURE, KOUTA?

......
ALL RIGHT. I'LL SPARE YOU **THIS TIME**. FOR KOUTA.

THANK YOU, KOUTA!
MY DEAR, DEAR KOUTA!

AND FOR YOU, YUYA...
I'VE GOT SOMETHING SPECIAL...
...JUST FOR...
?!
...YOU!

YOU TRICKED ME!

SHUT UP, YOU LITTLE BRAT!

UGH!

STUPID, KOUTA! HOW MANY TIMES HAVE I TOLD YOU?

THE WEAK SHALL LOSE...

...THE STRONG SURVIVE.

AND MERCY IS FOR FOOLS! HAHAHA HAA!

UNH...

UGH... MY EYES... BLURRY ...
I'VE GOT TO DO SOMETHING ...
...OR I'M DEAD!
THAT'S IT!
IT MUST BE TERRIFYING, GOING BLIND. HMMM... NOW, HOW SHOULD WE BEGIN THE TORTURE?
ばっ
YOU'LL HAVE TO AIM BETTER THAN THAT!
ばしゃあ
?!
AH! OH, GOD! WHAT'S THAT SMELL!
YOU BITCH! HOW DARE YOU DEFILE MY BODY WITH THAT SHIT!
DON'T THINK I'LL LET YOU DIE EASY!

AAAH!
AGH! GAH!
GUH!
WHERE ARE YOU SHOOTING, HMMM?
NO GOOD.
HEAD'S TOO FUZZY... CAN'T FEEL WHERE SHE IS...
GOTTA GET OUTSIDE...
OUTSIDE...
ガラガラガラ

?!
THAT SOUND! THE DOOR...?
ARE YOU OKAY, YUYA-SAN?
THAT VOICE ...

KYOSHIRO!

OOOOPS! SORRY I'M LATE. SEE, I WAS TIED UP IN THE TREE AND I...
Yuya-san tied me extra tight this time.
ばっ
HUH? Are you listening, Yuya-san?
STOP HER!
YOU'RE LETTING HER ESCAPE!
GET OUT OF MY WAY!
Y-YES, JOOH-SAMA!

LITTLE BITCH! DO YOU THINK YOU CAN WIN BECAUSE YOU'RE OUTSIDE?
!!
INSIDE...

OUTSIDE...
YOU'RE DEAD.

IF YOU BEG...
...MAYBE I'LL LET YOU CHOOSE HOW TO DIE.

SO SHE THINKS THAT SHE'LL BE ABLE TO HEAR ME BETTER OUTSIDE, EH? AS IF I'D BE SO FOOLISH...

...TO GIVE AWAY MY POSITION BY STEPPING ON LEAVES.

YOU CAN BE ASHAMED...
...OF YOUR STUPIDITY...
...IN HELL!
YUYA-SAN!

EH
...

HOW DID YOU...

THE PERFUME.
The one Kyoshiro gave me.

I COULDN'T TELL WHERE YOU WERE INSIDE BECAUSE YOUR STINK FILLED THE ENTIRE ROOM.
BUT OUTSIDE... WELL, THAT'S A WHOLE DIFFERENT STORY NOW, ISN'T IT?
If it's less than three jou, it's a sure thing.
I JUST WAITED... AND FOLLOWED MY NOSE.
I ...

I WASN'T REALLY GOING TO HURT YOU, DEAR YUYA! I JUST WANTED TO TEACH KOUTA ABOUT BEING STRONG, THAT'S ALL!
YOU WANT TO TEACH, KAZURA?

GO TEACH IN HELL.

YUYA-SAN! NO!

AH
HH
...
SEEMS
...
I'VE RUN OUT OF BULLETS.
...IT'S YOUR LUCKY DAY.
ほっ…

きゃきゃ

I'VE TOLD THE AUTHORITIES EVERYTHING, SO YOU'LL BE SAFE NOW.
YOU'LL HAVE TO TAKE CARE OF YOUR SISTER, BUT I KNOW YOU CAN DO IT.
EAT!

AHH... WHAT DO YOU CARE?

I DO CARE. VERY MUCH.
THERE'S NO SHAME IN BEING POOR, AND IT WILL BE DIFFICULT ...
...BUT YOU'RE A SPECIAL BOY, KOUTA.
AND ONE DAY, I KNOW YOU'LL GROW UP TO BE A SPECIAL MAN.
YOU HAVE A GOOD HEART, KOUTA. NEVER FORGET THAT.

AH ...
I KNOW.
かぁ...

GOOD!
LOOK AFTER TAE-CHAN.

WELL, TAKE CARE!
Bye! Byyyye! Onii-tan! Onee-tan!
......
ONII-TAN... I'M HUNGRY!
YEAH... LET'S EAT.
YAY!
HUH?
TAE? WHAT'S THAT? WHERE DID YOU GET IT?
FROM ONEE-TAN!
Heh-heh-heh

Nice to meet you!
I LEND YOU 3 SILVER.
Take care, Tae-chan!
NO INTEREST. NON-RETURNABLE.
Bye²

...

WHAT IS IT?
Something good?
NOTHING.

IT'S NOTHING ...

THAT WAS A VERY SWEET THING TO DO, YUYA-SAN.
I DON'T KNOW OF MANY BOUNTY HUNTERS WHO WOULD'VE DONE THE SAME IF THEY WERE IN YOUR SHOES.
It's true!
......
I'M STILL A LITTLE WORRIED ABOUT THOSE TWO.

ANY-WAY...

I'M SORRY I DIDN'T HELP!

Please don't sell me for the bounty!

I HAVE A FEELING THEY'LL BE JUST FINE.

WHAT?

WHAT'S THIS FOR?

YOUR PERFUME.

I GUESS SOMETIMES YOU ACTUALLY MAKE SOMETHING THAT'S USEFUL, HUH?

Today's the only time I'll say that.

YUYA-SAN...

LET'S GET THE HECK OUTTA HERE.

You can buy yourself something nice. Like your Ayame-chan.

WAIT FOR ME, YUYA-SAN!

IT'S STILL 5 MON SHORT!

I'M GLAD WE FOUND THIS PLACE BEFORE IT GOT DARK.
Otherwise we'd be camping again.
YUYA-SAN, I...
WHAT, KYO-SHIRO?
CHAPTER 11
CHERRY BLOSSOM AND CROW
YOU THINK MAYBE YOU COULD DUMP SOME OF YOUR STUFF?
WHAT?! A GIRL NEEDS HER ACCESSORIES!
SAMURAI DEEPER
KYO

I WONDER HOW THEY CLEARED THE MOUNTAIN TO BUILD THIS PLACE.
PLEASE DON'T BUY ANYTHING ELSE...
Here he is.
WHAT?
THIS IS A PUBLIC ROAD!
WHO DO YOU THINK YOU ARE, WALKING DOWN THIS ROAD?

NOT AS LONG AS WE'RE HERE, YOU SHRIVELED BITCH!
IF YOU WANT TO PASS...

...THEN GIVE US THE MOUN-TAIN!
NO!
THAT OLD LADY'S NOT AFRAID OF ANYONE!
ARE YOU JUST GOING TO STAND THERE...
...AND LET THEM RUN THIS TOWN?
...

THEY WON'T HELP YOU, YOU OLD BAG!
NO ONE WILL!

YOU CAN HELP! DO IT!
HUH ?!

YAAAAA!
HOW'D YOU GET BACK THERE ?!
DO IT! YOU CAN HELP!
NO! NO WAY!
C'MON, GUYS. FIGHTING NEVER SOLVED ANYTHING. AND SHE'S JUST AN OLD WOMAN...
Let's all be friends!

YEAH! YOU TELL 'EM!
Go on! Go on!
PLEASE, SHUT UP!
HEY ...
YOU CAN'T TELL US WHAT TO DO!
You wanna die?!
WAA AAH!
You've got it all wrong!

WHAT DO YOU THINK YOU'RE DOING? You dirtied my kimono.
I...
WHO THE HELL ARE YOU?!
WHY DON'T YOU PICK ON SOMEONE YOUR OWN SIZE? Guys like you make me sick.
WHAT? SHIT, GIRL!

WHAT?
GET LOST, BITCH!

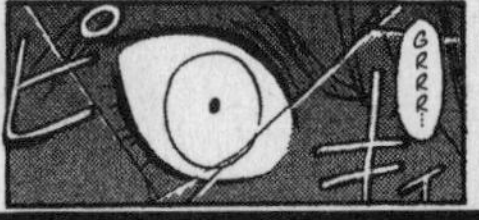
GRRR!

MIND YOUR OWN BUSINESS, YOU DUMB COW!
OKAY...

YOU APOLOGIZE TO ME NOW...
...AND I WON'T KICK YOUR ASS TOO BADLY.

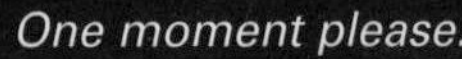
One moment please.

I SWEAR. SOME MEN JUST DON'T KNOW HOW TO SAY, "I'M SORRY." Their mouths are bigger than their fists.
UH... YUYA-SAN... THAT WAS...
What was that exactly...?
Doki
Doki

YOU'RE ONE TOUGH CHILD.
I'M NOT, REALLY.
WELL, THANK YOU JUST THE SAME. I INSIST, YOU STAY THE NIGHT WITH ME.
IF YOU SAY SO... THANK YOU...
ISN'T IT DIFFICULT LIVING IN THE MIDDLE OF NOWHERE ?
I prefer cities, myself.
NONSENSE. STAY AWHILE AND SEE. IT'S PARADISE HERE.
HMMM. NOT TO ME.
I MEAN, I'D LOVE TO HIKE HERE ONCE IN A WHILE, BUT...
My legs are already tired.
DON'T YOU AGREE, KYO-SHIRO?
SURE. WHAT-EVER.

SAY... BAA-CHAN, DO YOU THINK YOU COULD LIGHTEN YOUR LOAD A LITTLE?
It keeps getting bigger...
ぎぎぎぎ...
WHAT? A GIRL NEEDS HER ACCESSO-RIES!
THAT'S RIGHT.

YOU WANT TO HELP, TOO? THAT'S VERY KIND OF YOU.
I've got some food at my house.
OU...
IT... IT'S A REAL...
AAAAAAAAAA!

GYAAAAAA!
AAAA?!

......

?!
WHAT'S WRONG, KYOSHIRO?
HUH?
!!
OH...

...MY!...

A HUGE SAKURA TREE...

...IN FULL BLOOM.
In the wrong season?
SO BEAUTIFUL ...
...
COME ALONG. I'M SURE YOU'RE TIRED AFTER ALL THAT WALKING. COME ALONG INSIDE...

WHAT AN AMAZING CHERRY BLOSSOM TREE!
THAT MUST BE HOW THEY BLOOM IN HEAVEN.
I don't want to leave...
I'VE NEVER SEEN ONE SO LUSH.
MMMHMM. YOU YOUNG PEOPLE ALWAYS SAY THE SAME THING.
THAT TREE IS FILLED WITH MEMORIES OF ME AND MY HUSBAND.
WE MET UNDER THAT TREE...
FELL IN LOVE UNDER THAT TREE...
MADE LOVE UNDER THAT TREE. I WAS ONLY 14 AND HE WAS 17.
SINCE HE PASSED AWAY, THE TREE IS ALL I HAVE LEFT TO REMEMBER HIM BY.
HAH! NO WONDER IT'S SO BEAUTIFUL!
BAA-CHAN... WHEN YOU ARGUED WITH THOSE MEN, THEY SAID SOMETHING ABOUT A MOUNTAIN...
IS IT THIS MOUNTAIN?
AND WHO WERE THOSE THUGS?

THE TEA IS READY...
THANK YOU!
THOSE BUMS...
THEY'RE PART OF THE GANG THAT'S MOVED IN ON THIS TERRITORY.
THE KIDOU CLAN.

THEY'LL KILL ANYONE WHO STANDS IN THEIR WAY.
THEY'VE EXPANDED QUICKLY BEHIND THEIR RUTHLESS ASSASSINS...
...THE SAN SAI SHU-- THE THREE COLOR GANG.

THEY KILL WITHOUT MERCY. THEY KILL FOR PLEASURE. I DON'T LIKE TO THINK HOW MANY POOR PEASANTS AND WOODCUTTERS DIED BEFORE THEM.
OH MY...
...
THOSE THUGS HAVE SCARED EVERYONE OFF THE MOUNTAIN.
EVERYONE BUT ME, THAT IS.

I'LL NEVER LEAVE THIS MOUNTAIN. THEY'LL HAVE TO KILL ME...

...BEFORE I LEAVE MY MEMORIES.

BAA-CHAN...
...

SPEAK OF THE DEVIL, AND HERE HE IS!
Heh-heh!
WHO THE--?!

HUH?
NOBODY'S THERE...
WHO ARE YOU LOOKING FOR?
EVERYBODY ...
花鳥風月

WHAT?!
HOW DID YOU--?!
はっ
ALLOW ME TO INTRODUCE MYSELF. I AM WHITE CROW OF THE THREE COLOR GANG.
And now that we all know each other...
I HAVE BUSINESS TO DISCUSS WITH THE OLD WOMAN.
HE WAS RIGHT BEHIND US AND I NEVER EVEN KNEW. WHO... WHAT... IS HE?
HEY! OLD BITCH!
YOU WANNA SHAME ME IN PUBLIC!
WELL COME KISS YOUR DAMN TREE GOOD-BYE!
NO! YOU BEAST!
PLEASE DON'T!

SEE WHAT HAPPENS ...
STOP, DAMN YOU!
PLEASE! NO!
...WHEN YOU SCREW WITH US!
HOW DISGUSTING.
HUH?

NO ONE TOUCHES THE CHERRY TREE...
HEY!
WHA-?! WHITE CROW-SAMA?! WE DIDN'T KNOW YOU WERE--
WHY DID YOU --?
SUCH BEAUTY SHOULD NEVER BE DESTROYED. UNDERSTAND?
UH... SURE...
...

HE KILLED ONE OF HIS OWN MEN WITHOUT A THOUGHT! SUCH CRUELTY!

I'M SORRY YOU HAD TO SEE SUCH A MESS...

... OBAA-SAMA.

THIS IS YOUR LAST NOTICE. YOU HAVE THREE DAYS TO LEAVE THE MOUNTAIN. PLEASE GO. OTHERWISE...

...THE THREE COLOR GANG WILL RETURN TO SEE YOU OFF PERSONALLY.

HAVE I MADE MYSELF CLEAR?

AGAIN... SORRY FOR THE MESS.
HAVE A NICE DAY.
S-SO CRUEL...

HE'S ONE OF THE GUYS HARASSING YOU?!
I'M AFRAID SO...
Y-Y-Y-Y-YUYA-SAN! WE'VE GOTTA GET OUTTA HERE!
THREE COLOR GANG ...
CRUEL, MERCILESS ASSASSINS. THEY'LL KILL ANYONE. WOMEN. CHILDREN. THERE'S A BOUNTY FOR THEM, YOU KNOW...
YUYA'S BOUNTY BOOK
ポン
THEY'RE WORTH 100 RYO EACH.
BAA-CHAN, WHY DO THEY WANT YOUR MOUNTAIN?
....
I DON'T KNOW... MAYBE BECAUSE OF THE TREASURE ?
THERE'S A *LEGEND* THAT'S BEEN PASSED DOWN IN MY FAMILY FROM GENERATION TO GENERATION.
WHILE ESCAPING TO HIRAIZUMI, PRINCE YOSHITSUNE MINAMOTO BURIED HIS **TREASURE** SOMEWHERE IN THIS MOUNTAIN.
THEY SAY THERE'S ENOUGH GOLD HERE TO BUILD THREE CASTLES.

TRE... TRE... TRE... TREASURE?!
Three castles?!
Doki Doki Doki Doki
YUYA-SAN! WE'VE GOT TO GO! I'LL CARRY ALL YOUR STUFF! I PROMISE!
PLEASE!
OH, OBAA-SAMA...
DO YOU NEED A YOJIMBO?
ARRRGH!
I knew she'd ask something like that!
Doki Doki
HUH?

Kyoshiro and Yuya met an **old woman** who lived beneath a stunning **cherry blossom tree**– a tree, which held all the memories of her life with her dead husband.

The woman and the tree live atop a mountain in which, according to legend, the fabulous **treasure** of Prince Yoshitsune Minamoto is buried.

The greedy **Kidou clan** hired **the Three Colors Gang** to force the inhabitants off the mountain using whatever means necessary.

Once Yuya heard the story of the treasure and the old woman's plight...

CHAPTER 12 POISON OF SNAKE AND SCORPION

OH, OBAA-SAMA... DO YOU NEED A YOJIMBO?

ちゃ♡

ARRRGH! I KNEW SHE WAS GONNA SAY THAT!

SAMURAI DEEPER KYO

I AM THE BOUNTY HUNTRESS YUYA SHIINA. MANY PEOPLE SAY I'M THE BEST ON TOKAIDO-CHU! I'M SURE YOU'VE HEARD OF ME...
I PROMISE TO PROTECT YOU, OBAA-SAMA!
I...I AM...?
WOW...
I NEVER KNEW...
I HAVE NO MONEY TO PAY YOU...
DON'T BE SILLY!
I THINK IT'S THE YOUNGER GENERATION'S RESPONSIBILITY TO CARE FOR THE ELDERLY.
YOU'RE OUR NATIONAL TREASURES, AFTER ALL!
TREASURE! TREASURE! TREASURE! YEP! YOU'RE JUST OUR LITTLE TREASURE!
AND... UH... SPEAKING OF TREASURE...
HERE WE GO.
WHERE DO YOU THINK THAT SILLY SAMURAI YOSHITSUNE HID HIS?
HE DIDN'T.
GAG!
I MEAN... IT IS ONLY A LEGEND.

BUT...
A LEGEND WILL HAVE SOME TRUTH...
MMMM. I SUPPOSE. BUT IT WAS SO LONG AGO. HUNDREDS OF YEARS.
I DON'T KNOW WHY EVERYBODY SEEMS TO THINK I KNOW WHERE IT IS.
BUT I SUPPOSE AS LONG AS THE KIDOU CLAN THINKS THAT, THEY WON'T HURT ME.
イッヒヒッヒッ
THEY MAY BE YOUNG AND TOUGH...
...BUT THAT'S NO MATCH FOR AGE AND WISDOM.
HA HA HA HA HA HA!
O... OBAA-SAMA!
THERE IS SO MUCH I CAN LEARN FROM YOU!
WELL, YOU DO SEEM TO HAVE THE MAKINGS OF A FINE LADY. YOUR GOOD LOOKS REMIND ME OF ME WHEN I WAS YOUR AGE...
REALLY?
NOW'S MY CHANCE!
シュルルル
NOT SO FAST!
S... SORRY!

BAA-CHAN... WHO IS THIS?

!

...

UH... THAT WAS MY SON...

BUT...

...THIRTY YEARS AGO...

IT'S VERY WINDY TONIGHT.
CHERRY BLOSSOM PETALS DANCING ON THE NIGHT BREEZE CAN BE SO BEAUTIFUL...
SUCH A POET, GENMA-SAMA!
BUT THE SEASON OF THE CHERRY BLOSSOM IS OVER, SO THERE WILL BE NO MORE THIS YEAR.
hee hee
......
GENMA-SAMA...

HEY! WHEN DID YOU...
WHITE CROW?
DON'T FORGET ABOUT ME. BLACK SCORPION IS ALSO HERE.
KYA AH!
WHITE CROW? DID YOU SEE HER?
YES.
I GAVE HER THREE DAYS. SHE IS THE LAST ONE ON THE MOUNTAIN.
YOU ARE TOO COURTEOUS, WHITE CROW! YOUR KINDNESS WILL BE YOUR UNDOING!
GENMA-DONO!
CALM DOWN, BLACK SCORPION! WHITE CROW HAS THE FLOOR ...

NO... AND YET...I HAVE AN UNEASY FEELING ABOUT THE BOY.
I CAN'T PUT A FINGER ON IT, BUT THERE'S SOMETHING ABOUT HIS SMELL...

THE OLD WOMAN HAS TWO GUESTS.
DID YOU KNOW THEM?
SO?! JUST GET RID OF ALL OF THEM!

GEN-MA-SAMA?
WHAT?

AND THOSE EYES...
THEY ALMOST MADE ME FEEL... NERVOUS.

HA HA HA! WHY DON'T YOU JUST ADMIT IT?! YOU'RE AFRAID OF A LITTLE BOY! YOU BRING SHAME ON THE THREE COLORS GANG!
DON'T WORRY! I'LL SNAP HIS NECK FOR YOU!

I SEE. EVEN YOU, THE ONE CALLED *"ICE FLAME"* FOR YOUR COOL DEMEANOR, ARE LEFT UNSETTLED?

...
JUST GIVE ME THE ORDER, GENMA-DONO!
IF THAT IS WHAT YOU WISH, BLACK SCORPION, THEN SO BE IT.
ANY OBJECTIONS, WHITE CROW?
...
I'LL SHOW YOU, GENMA-DONO!
WATCH AND LEARN, WHITE CROW! HA HA HA HA HA!
GENMA-SAMA...
HUSH, WHITE.
I HAVE TO GIVE HIM A CHANCE, TOO. OTHERWISE, HE GOES QUITE MAD.
IF HE SHOULD FAIL, YOU MAY GO AFTER HIM. IS THAT CLEAR?
YES.
AND WHAT HAPPENED TO RED TIGER?
WELL ...

DISAPPEARED AGAIN. AS USUAL, I DON'T KNOW WHAT'S IN HIS HEAD.
THEY PLAY SO LOUD.
WE'LL I GUESS THINGS ARE ABOUT TO GET INTEREST-ING...

C'MON, OBAA-CHAN! GIMME A BREAK! IT'S TOO EARLY FOR THIS!
NOPE.
C'MON! C'MON! PICK UP THE WOOD!
ACK!
WHY'RE YOU SO ROUGH?
ROUGH? YUYA SAID I HAD TO KEEP YOU IN LINE! SHOW YOU WHO'S BOSS!
YAAH!
BUT SHE DIDN'T SAY TO KILL ME!
LEAVE HER BE! SHE'S GOTTA GET READY FOR THE KIDOU CLAN.
OH? I THOUGHT SHE WAS JUST DIGGING FOR TREASURE.
WHO, ME?

OKAY! THAT'S THE LAST BUNDLE.
AHH HH!
HERE. HAVE SOME WATER.
THANKS.
...

WHAT'S WRONG?
Something on my face?
NOTHING IT'S JUST... sorry.
YOU REMIND ME...
...OF MY SON WHO DISAPPEARED.

HE WAS NEVER DEVOTED TO HIS FATHER AND ME... AND NOW HE'S GONE...
BA... BAA-CHAN ...

BAA-CHAN! IF I CAN HELP YOU IN ANY WAY, JUST ASK! OKAY?
I know I'm not good enough, but...
YOU ...

YOU ARE SO SWEET.
IF YOU INSIST ...

JUST CARRY THIS BACK TO MY HOUSE.
GUH!

I CAN'T DO THIS BY MYSELF!
HOW NICE SOME YOUNG PEOPLE CAN BE!

HEE HEE HEE! SEE YOU AT HOME!
WAIT !
DON'T DAWDLE!
すたたん

DAMN.

SHIT!
WHERE'S THAT DUMB BEAR WHEN I NEED HIM?
OH! DAMMIT!
THAT OLD WOMAN IS SCARY...
All women are the same.
?!
WAH!
WHAT ?!
NEEDLES ?!
THAT WAS LUCKY, BOY, TO AVOID ALL MY KOUTETSU SEN. LET'S SEE YOU BLOCK ME AGAIN...

THIS TIME, YOU'LL NEED MORE THAN LUCK...
...TO STOP BLACK SCORPION!
Y...
YOU'RE FROM THE THREE COLOR GANG!
HUH?
I'M JUST COLLECTING FIREWOOD! I HAVEN'T DONE ANYTHING!
YOU SCARED WHITE CROW, AND THAT'S ENOUGH!
GET HIM!

KYAAAAAH!
HAAA!
YAA AA!
DIEEE!

STOP SQUIRMING!

UGH!
...
PLEASE STOP!
SHUT UP AND STAND STILL!

MEN ...

DON'T WORRY, BLACK SCORPION-SAMA! WE'LL FINISH HIM!

DAMN, HE'S FAST!
ARE YOU GUYS THROUGH YET?
AH HA HA!
YOU CAN'T DODGE US FOREVER!

EH?

BUT... YOU KILLED THEM...

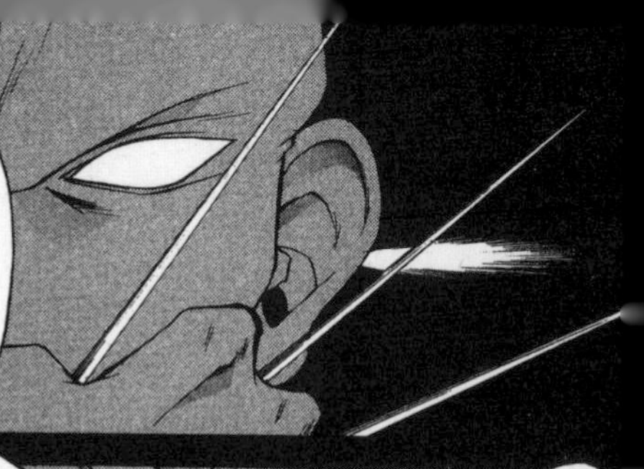
PATHETIC. SUCH IS THE PRICE OF FAILURE.

NO ONE CAN ESCAPE THE DEATH MY KOUTETSU SEN BRING.
EVEN IF YOU DON'T DIE FROM THE PIERCING NEEDLE, ONE OF THE FOUR POISONS WHICH COAT IT WILL FINISH YOU OFF.
THE FIRST IS ***ATSU SHI***, THE "FEVER DEATH," WHICH BURNS YOUR INSIDES LIKE ARSENIC. THE SECOND IS ***YUMEMI SHI***, THE "DREAM DEATH", MADE FROM THE ASHITAKE BENI MUSHROOM, WHICH FILLS YOUR MIND WITH WAKING NIGHTMARES.
THE THIRD IS CALLED ***EMI SHI***, THE "SMILE DEATH." STRYCHNINE FROM THE MACHIN SEEDS WILL LEAVE YOUR BODY CRAMPED AND IN AGONY, SO WHEN DEATH FINALLY RELEASES YOU, YOU CANNOT HELP BUT SMILE.

....
OR PERHAPS...
...YOU'D PREFER ***SHI GYOKU***, THE "EXTREME DEATH." A POISON OF MY OWN DESIGN, IT WILL MELT YOUR SKIN, FLESH AND BONES!
GYAAAH!
GASP!

SO, BOY, WHICH SHALL IT BE?
OR WOULD YOU RATHER I CHOOSE?
ばっ
GET AWAY FROM ME!
?!
WHAT?! WHEN DID YOU THROW THEM!?
!!
I CAN'T MOVE!
GET...

...READY!

YOU CAN'T ESCAPE ...
GET READY!
I CAN'T MOVE!
YAAAAAH!
SAMURAI DEEPER KYO
CHAPTER 13
EVIL EYES APPEAR

HEH. STUPID BIG-MOUTHED BRAT.

THERE'S YOUR SCARY KID, CROW, HANGING FROM A TREE! YOU REALLY HAVE LOST YOUR EDGE IF YOU WERE FRIGHTENED BY THAT. HA HA HA HA HA!
...
GET AWAY FROM ME!
DON'T LOOK BACK OR I'M DEAD!

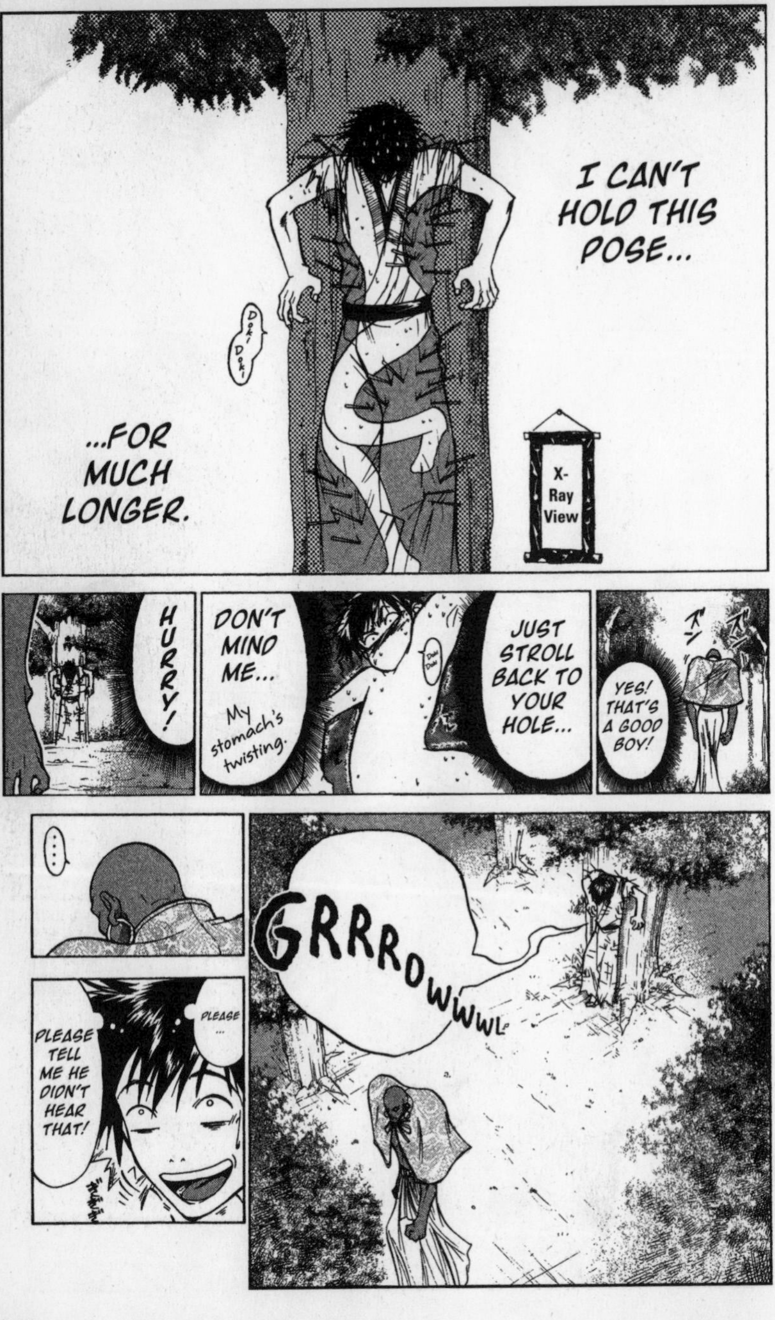

I CAN'T HOLD THIS POSE...

Doki Doki

...FOR MUCH LONGER.

X-Ray View

DIE, YOU LITTLE SHIT!
!!!
GYAAAH!
ポッ
ズ
カッ
UH... HI...
YOU ANNOYING... LITTLE...
THIS TIME...
...I WON'T MISS!
WAAAAAAAH!
ブチ Buchi
ブチ Buchi
ブチ Buchi
ブチ Buchi

RUN AWAY!
Lucky!
YOU WON'T ESCAPE!

I CAN'T KEEP LIVING LIKE THIS!

HUH?
THAT SOUND... A RIVER! I CAN HIDE UNDERWATER!
I'LL BE SAFE!
HUH?

A WATERFALL?!
IF I JUMP FROM THIS HEIGHT, I'LL GO KERSPLAT!
Things have gone from bad to worse...
Here he is.
30 Jou (90 meters)

WHAT'S WRONG? NO PLACE TO RUN?

GO AHEAD. JUMP. YOU'LL HAVE MORE OF A CHANCE THAN YOU WILL FACING ME!
...

?!

THERE'S NO REASON TO STRUGGLE.

C'MON. TURN AROUND AND DIE LIKE A MAN!

SHUT UP!
?!
WHAT'S...
WHAT?!
...HAPPENING TO HIM?!

COME GET ME.
DO YOU KNOW WHO YOU'RE TALKING TO?
FOOL!
WHAT?!

COME SEE HOW HARD IT IS TO KILL DEMON EYES KYO.

DEMON EYES KYO?!
IMPOSSIBLE! HE'S KILLED OVER 1,000 PEOPLE!

DEMON EYES KYO...

Why the left hand?

IS THIS WHAT HE LOOKED LIKE?

Shake ドキ ドキ Shake

ドキ Shake

THAT'S RIGHT. RUN. DEMON EYES KYO IS TOO STRONG!! YOU CAN'T BEAT HIM!! YOU'LL DIE!

BUT IN THE MEANTIME, YUYA-SAN SHOULD BE WONDERING WHY I'M SO LATE AND WILL LOOK FOR ME!!

C'MON, YUYA-SAN! HURRY UP AND SAVE ME!

PLEASE GIVE UP!
And please come quick, Yuya-san!
DEMON EYES KYO, HUH? I MUST ADMIT, I'M A BIT SURPRISED.
Still the left-hand.
doki
doki
HE... HE GAVE UP?!
He lowered his hand.
I...

I'VE BEEN WANTING TO FIGHT YOU FOR SOME TIME!
I can't stop shaking!

UH...HE'S GETTING A LITTLE TOO EXCITED ABOUT THIS...
And he's got twice as many needles!
C'MON, KYO! LET'S GO!
TOO FAST! I CAN'T DODGE!

WHAT?!
HOW...
HEH...
HEH HEH HEH...IS THAT THE BEST YOU CAN DO? NOW I'LL SHOW YOU MY OUGI... MY TECHNIQUE.
C'MON, YOU BIG JERK! BUY THE LIE...
...AND LEAVE ME THE HELL ALONE!
HEH HEH HEH... GOOD.
WHAT?

OKAY THEN, LET ME SHOW YOU MY ULTIMATE OGI...
YOU CAN STOP TEN KOUTETSU SEN, BUT WHAT ABOUT A THOUSAND?
DON'T EXAG-GERATE!
I THINK HE'S SERIOUS!
?!
WHY ARE YOU DROPPING YOUR...
GUH ...

GUUUUUUOOOOOH!
OH... SHIT!
Buru
Buru

GOOHOOOOH!
Buru
Buru
HIS OUGI...

AMATA SHIGYKU!
WAAAAAAH!

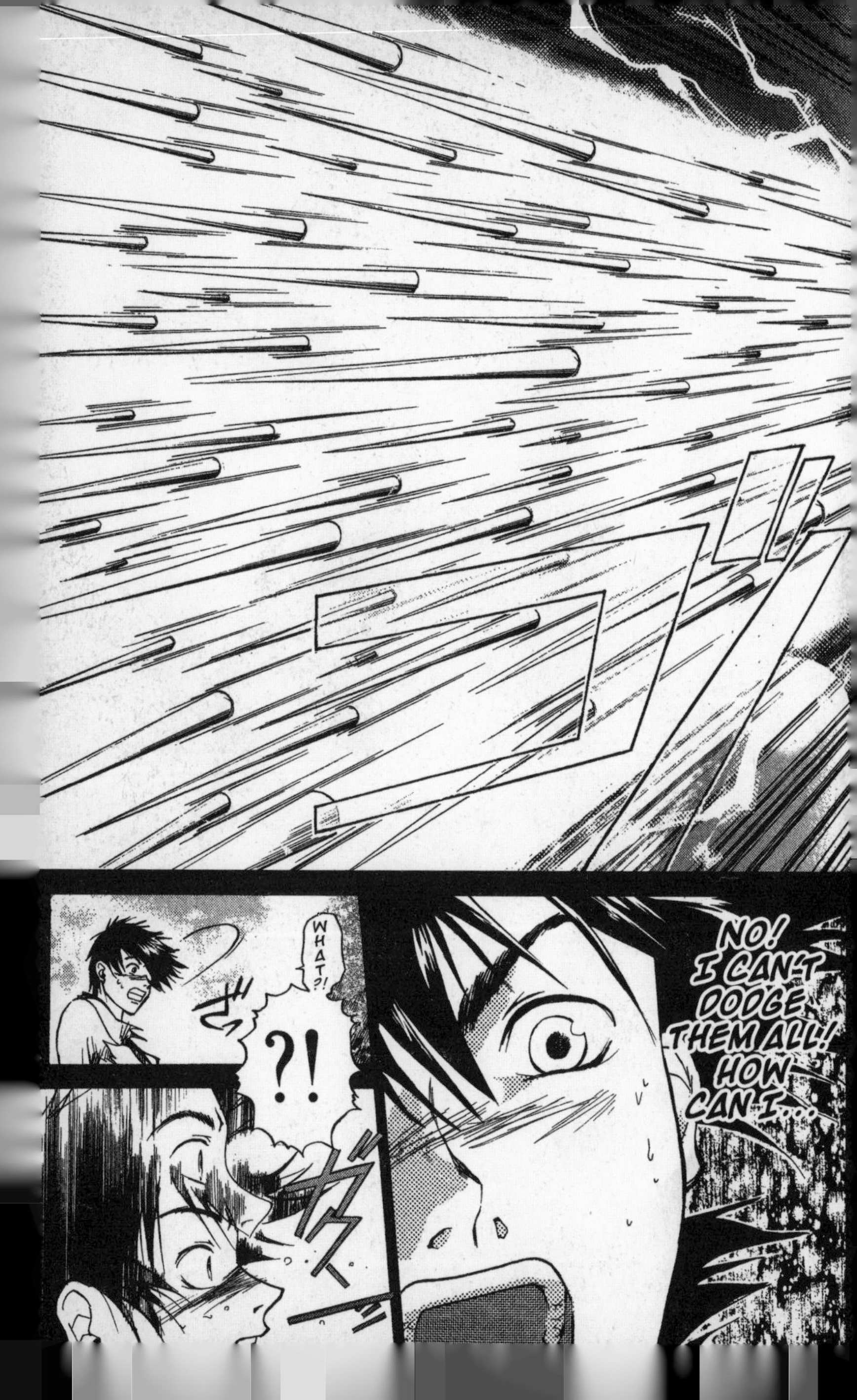
NO! I CAN'T DODGE THEM ALL! HOW CAN I...
WHAT?!
?!

EH?
YAAAAAAAAA!

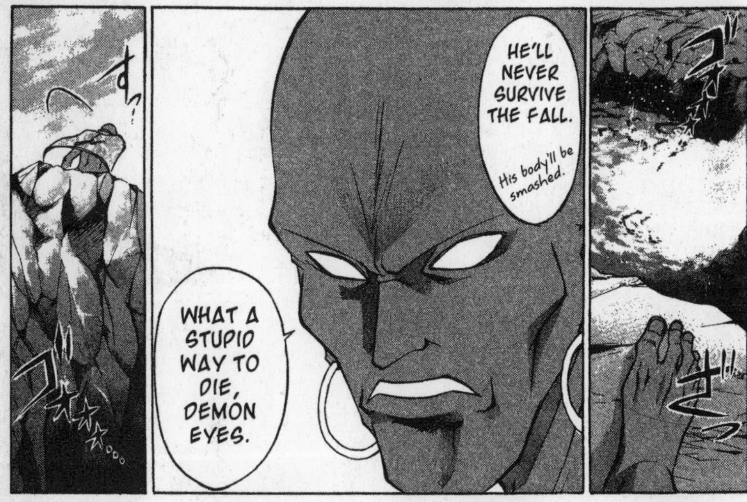
HE'LL NEVER SURVIVE THE FALL.
His body'll be smashed.
WHAT A STUPID WAY TO DIE, DEMON EYES.

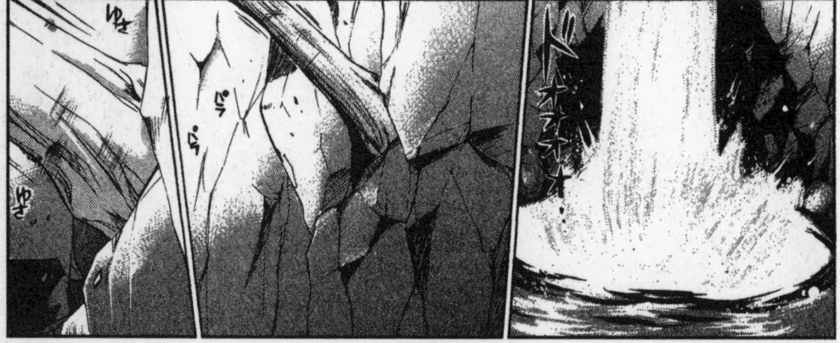

AM I LUCKY, OR WHAT?
OR... MAYBE NOT...

THE TREE WAS IN THE PERFECT SPOT.
What a fluke...
どどどど…
HOW THE HELL AM I GONNA GET DOWN FROM HERE?
I'm glad I was caught, but...
するする
!!
A ROPE?!
I really am lucky.
I KNEW I SHOULDN'T WORRY! YUYA-SAN CAME!
がしっ

SO LUCKY!
FINALLY!
I MADE IT!
ざっ

THANK YOU, YUYA-SAN!
That was easier than I expected!
HUH?
Hairy legs?
LOOKS LIKE YOU OWE ME BIG-TIME...
...DEMON EYES KYO.
WHO ARE YOU?!

Three Color Gang Unite!

THIS HAS NOTHING TO DO WITH ANYTHING. IT'S ABOUT MY **PEN NAME**.

I'M OFTEN ASKED BY FRIENDS, "WHY DO YOU USE THAT PEN NAME?"

IN FACT, IT'S A NAME MY PARENTS CAME UP WITH WHEN I WAS BORN, BUT THEY NEVER USED IT.

...WHAT COMPLICATED PARENTS.

Genma, the head of the Kidou clan, hired the **Three Color Gang** to drive out the townspeople.

The trouble started when Yuya and Kyoshiro became yojimbo to an old woman who lived at the foot of a mountain; the same mountain where legend says Prince Yoshitsune Minamoto buried his treasure.

Genma wanted the legendary treasure for himself. Black Scorpion attacked Kyoshiro to prove he was better and stronger than White Crow.

Black Scorpion

White Crow

Red Tiger

Kyoshiro managed to hold Black Scorpion at bay, until he fell off a cliff.

HOW THE HELL AM I GONNA GET DOWN FROM HERE? I'm glad I was caught, but...

A ROPE!!

IT MUST BE YUYA-SAN! So easy!

I MADE IT!

THANKS, YUYA-SAN! Huh?

SAMURAI DEEPER KYO

WHO ARE YOU?!

SAMURAI DEEPER
KYO
CHAPTER 14
THE THIRD ONE

I'M GLAD YA MADE IT...
かっ
に
...BUT I THINK YA OWE ME, DEMON EYES KYO.
AND YOU ARE? ...
!
YOU SURVIVED A DIFFICULT FIGHT.
DAMN RIGHT, I DID!
Thanks for mentioning it.
AND IT WASN'T ALL LUCK!
NO... NO...OF COURSE IT WASN'T.
THIS HUGE GUY JUST STROLLED UP TO ME AND...
GO ON...
HE LOOKED LIKE THIS!
His name was Black Lizard or Dark Toad or something.
BLACK SCORPION?
YEAH! YEAH! THAT'S HIS NAME!
Bingo!
...
ばっ
?!
HEY... HOW'D YOU KNOW HIS NAME?
...

HERE. THIS ONE'S FER YOU.
HUH?
BUT THIS ROCK MAY BE IN THE WAY...
Ain't that a shame...
UH... EXCUSE ME...
Are you even listening to me?
IF YOU'RE THINKING I'M ONE OF THE THREE COLOR GANG...
...YOU'RE RIGHT.
YOU GOT A PROBLEM WITH THAT?
No complaints, right?
I KNEW IT!
WELL, THANKS FOR THE HELP. I'LL JUST GO BACK NOW AND HANG FROM THE TREE...
We'll just pretend that the last 5 pages never happened.
WAIT.
LET ME GUESS. YOU WON'T LET ME GO?
PLEASE...
WHAT?
JUST ONE TIME, PLEASE?
WHAT?!

SPAR WITH ME JUST THIS ONCE!
IT'S THE LEAST YOU CAN DO AFTER I SAVED YOU!
Please? I'm begging!
SPAR... WITH THIS LOG STAFF?
YEAH, THAT'S RIGHT. IT'S SIMPLE.
FIRST ONE TO GET KNOCKED OUT OR STEP OUT-OF-BOUNDS LOSES. IT'S JUST A GAME, SEE?!
AND IF YOU WIN, THEN I'LL OWE YOU A FAVOR.
IS HE SERIOUS?
SO...
THIS GUY SEEMS DIFFERENT FROM THE OTHER TWO. AND IT IS JUST A GAME...
If it's dangerous, I can always run...
HE DOESN'T LOOK SO STRONG, EITHER...
WELL... WHAT THE HECK.
REALLY?!
Great!
LET ME JUST MOVE THIS ROCK FIRST...
SURE...
You go right ahead.

HOI!
Hyotsu!

APPEARANCES CAN BE DECEIVING-- HE'S A MONSTER!!!
I'm so stupid!
AAAAAAH!

WELL THEN...
...KYO-HAN.

....

I'LL GO FIRST!

ドゴオー
I DID IT!
I KILLED DEMON EYES KYO!
WHAT DO YOU SAY NOW, WHITE CROW!? WHO IS THE MASTER?!
YOU ARE THE MASTER OF NOISE, BLACK SCORPION. NOTHING MORE.
BAH! YOU'RE JUST JEALOUS BECAUSE I KILLED DEMON EYES KYO AND YOU RAN AWAY!
DEMON EYES... ?!

THAT WAS YOUR BOY, CROW, AND I KILLED HIM!! THE LEGENDARY KILLER OF A THOUSAND PEOPLE, DEMON EYES KYO!!
HMM... THERE WAS SOMETHING I...

SOMETHING THAT SCARED THE HELL OUTTA YOU, YOU MEAN!
WHERE'S HIS HEAD?
IT'S GONE! HE FELL OFF A CLIFF. BUT HE'S DEAD, DAMN YOU!
I DUNNO. BRINGING BACK THE HEAD IS ONE OF THE BASICS OF OUR BUSINESS.
No head, no proof.
WHAT?
WHAT DID YOU DO WITH DEMON EYES' HEAD?
You do have it, don't you...?

D-DON'T GIVE ME THAT SHIT!
I DON'T NEED TO PROVE A DAMN THING TO YOU! SINCE WHEN DID YOU BECOME OUR BOSS?!

I'M TIRED OF TAKING ORDERS FROM YOU AND GENMA!
NOBODY CAN STOP ME! I SHOULD BE THE BOSS!
What are you planning, White Crow?
YOU'RE A DISGRACE, BLACK SCORPION.
NOW STOP HOWLING. YOU MAY BE A FOOL...
...BUT YOU'RE NO ANIMAL.
YOU...
YOU!

AH ... AH ...
SUCH AN OAF...
IF YOU WANT TO KILL ME...
...COME QUIETLY.
KU ...
ACCORDING TO MY REPORTS, YOUR DEMON EYES KYO IS ALIVE...
...AND PLAYING A GAME WITH RED TIGER.
SO FOOLISH ...
....

huff
huff
huff
huff
huff
huff
huff
huff
huff
YOU AIN'T PUTTING UP MUCH OF A FIGHT.
BEFORE I FAINT...
WHY IS THAT?
...I'LL BE KILLED!
WELL, LET'S SEE HOW YOU HANDLE THIS.
EH?!

WHAT ?!
GAH !
EK !
URK !
HOW 'BOUT THIS?
!
SO FAST!
Deadly!
GUH!
AAH!
ばっ
GUH !
...

I'M GETTING PISSED...

Why can't I hit you?

* The tattoos on Red Tiger's Fingers read 1-8, from right to left.

...SPICE THINGS UP?
JUST FOR YOU, KYO-HAN.
?!
CRAP ...
I DON'T THINK I'M GOING TO LIKE THIS!
HERE GOES!
W-WHERE ...
ばっ
HERE ...
WHAT?!

HERE.
HERE.
HERE.

HERE I AM. RIGHT HERE.
AND HERE.
WHAT?!

HA HA HA HA HA!
YOU LOOK SURPRISED.
WHAT'S THE MATTER?
NOW YOU KNOW WHY MY NICKNAME IS...
KAGE BOUSHI, THE CRIMSON SHADOW.

WAAAH!

WITH THAT FOOL KYOSHIRO PUT AWAY, I'M BACK, I'M BAD AND HERE TO STAY! UNLESS YOU WANT MY BLADE IN YOUR BELLY, YOU'LL COME BACK FOR SAMURAI DEEPER VOLUME 3, AVAILABLE OCTOBER 2003.
And Ugly back there will give you the usual fan service.
....
UGLY?! THAT STUPID... GOOD-FOR-NOTHING... ARROGANT...
SAMURAI DEEPER
AKIMINE KAMIJYO

SPECIAL THANKS

YUZU HARUNO
HAZUKI ASAMI
SHINZIN ASHI 1430GOH
TAKAYA NAGAO
SHO YASHIOKA

AND
YOU

GLOSSARY

Buke – The samurai/warrior class. Can also refer to a specific samurai family.

Daikan – A magistrate. A local government administrator.

Daimyo – A feudal lord.

Edo – The new capital of Japan after Sekigahara, where the Shogun resides. Present-day Tokyo. To keep better control over the Daimyo, the shogun required that they spend every other year residing in Edo. With so much power centralized there, Edo quickly became one of the worlds' great cities.

Edo Era – (1603-1868) Japan's "golden era" of political and economic stability following the civil wars of the Sengoku era. Samurai Deeper Kyo takes place at the start of the Edo Era.

Iai – The art of sword drawing. Compared to western fencing, where swordplay involves a great deal of feinting, parrying, and movement, the Japanese tradition of swordplay is based around killing quickly and efficiently. The very act of drawing a sword is designed to be deadly.

Kansai-ben – Red Tiger speaks in the Kansai-ben, a fast-paced and slangy dialect from Japan's Kansai region (Kobe, Kyoto, Osaka). Red Tiger's way of calling people –han instead of –san is a trait of the dialect. Sometimes Kansai-ben is indicated in English with a southern accent.

Maai – The distance between two sword fighters. Without enough maii, a swordsman can't take a proper swing. Too much maii and a hit can't connect with sufficient force.

Mon – A small silver coin or copper coin.

Ochiudo – A fugitive samurai. Considered to be a rebel or a brigand.

(O)baa-san – An affectionate term for a grandmother or an older woman.

(O)neechan & (O)niichan – Affectionate terms for big sister and big brother.

Ryo – A gold coin of about 15 grams.

Sekigahara – The greatest battle in Japanese history which took place in fall of 1600 and ended the years of civil war in Japan. Following Sekigahara, all Japan would be ruled by one Shogun.

Sengoku Era – A time of civil war in Japan that lasted from 1467-1568. It was a warlike age—the heyday of the Samurai.

Shogun – The supreme ruler during Edo era Japan. The Shogun resides in the new capital of Edo and oversees the various Daimyo.

Tokaido-chu – The main trade road that runs along Japan's coast.

Tougun – The Eastern army during Sekigahara, allied with Ieyasu Tokugawa, the future Shogun.

Yojimbo – A bodyguard.

HONORIFICS GUIDE

Samurai Deeper Kyo retains the name suffixes from the original Japanese. In Japanese language there are a number of suffixes (also called "honorifics") which come after the name and indicate a level of respect between two people. Here is a listing of Japanese honorifics, many of which you'll see used in *Samurai Deeper Kyo.*

-san – The most common suffix. The equivalent of Mr. or Mrs.

-sama – Indicates a great level of respect or admiration and is used towards people who are older or of much higher standing.

-chan – Indicates friendly familiarity. -chan is usually used towards girls, but can sometimes apply to boys or adults.

-kun – The equivalent of -chan, -kun is usually reserved for boys.

-dono – Indicates great respect and formality. The equivalent of "sir" or "lord."

-jo – A formal way of addressing girls of high standing. Equivalent to Miss.

-joshi – A formal way of addressing young women of high standing. Equivalent to Ms.

-sensei – The term for teacher. It can also apply to someone who is a mentor figure or a master of a trade.

-senpai – In school, a term for upperclassmen. It can also apply to anyone in an organization who is older or more experienced.

O- Adding "O" in front of a term adds an extra level of respect. Calling an old wom "Obaa-sama" is a very formal address, but calling that person "baa-chan" implies a friendly, casual relationship.

BULLETIN BOARD

CHALLENGE AKIMINE KAMIJYO!

Think you can draw better than the manga-ka? Then send us your illustrations of Kyo!

We'll publish them in upcoming volumes, along with fan art from Japanese readers. Illustrations should be drawn in ink in black and white on clean, unlined paper.

Send mail to:
TOKYOPOP
5900 Wilshire Blvd., Ste. 2000
Los Angeles, CA 90036
Attn: *Samurai Deeper KYO* Fan Mail

You can also send your questions for Kamijyo-san or the TOKYOPOP editors!